This book belongs to:

_____

Read and spell every day.

A little bit of practice goes a very long way.

My Reading Chart

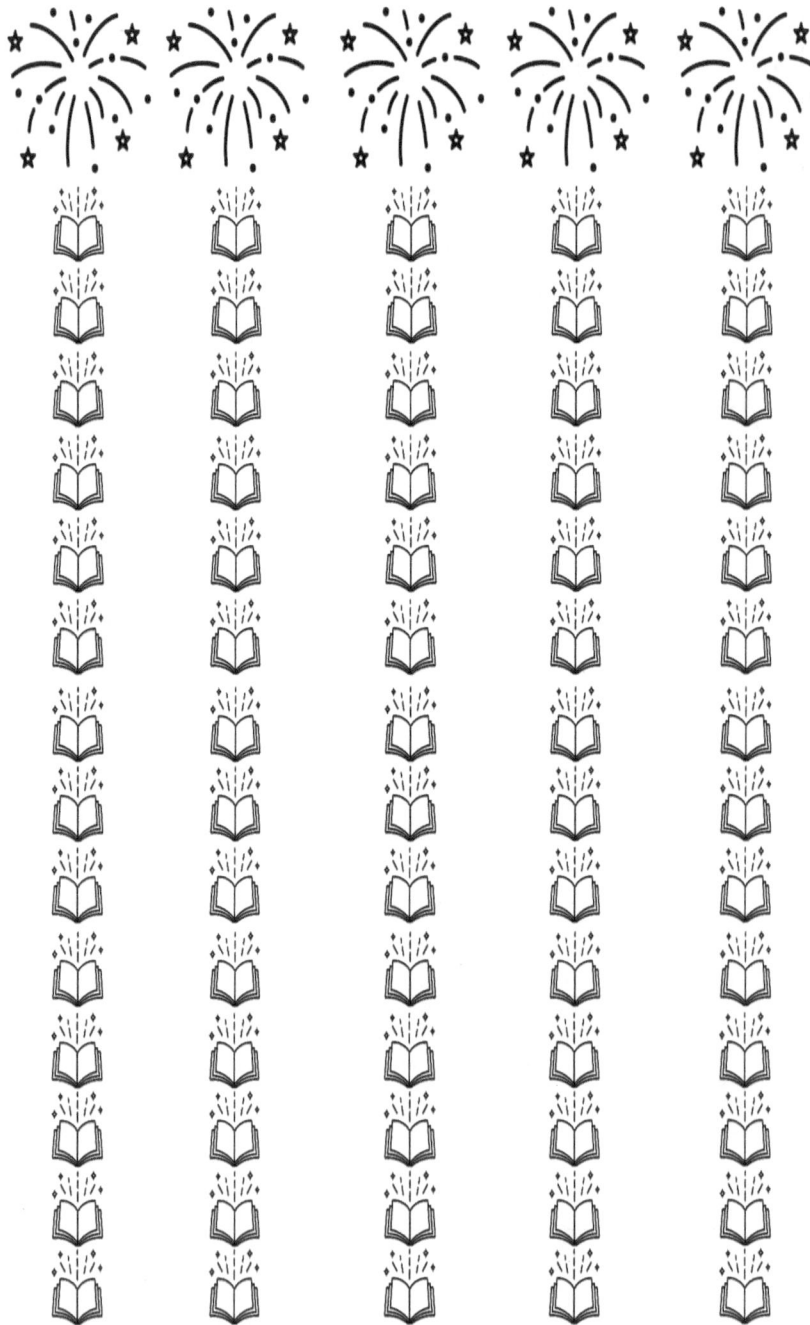

www.ingramcontent.com/pod-product-compliance
Lightning Source LLC
Chambersburg PA
CBHW030308100526
44590CB00012B/560